My Birthday Party

Written by
Barrie Wade

Photographed by
Chris Fairclough

W
FRANKLIN WATTS
LONDON • SYDNEY

Barrie Wade

"I love sharing stories with children. I think children are brilliant writers."

Chris Fairclough

"I've been taking photos for books for almost 30 years and have visited 53 countries. Every day is different!"

Mum and Dad said I could have a party for my birthday.

First Danny helped me to write the invitations.

Then Dad helped me to deliver them.

Next we
made lots of
party food.

9

Naveena,
Isabel, Idel
and Lily
came to
my party.

10

11

I gave them party hats.

They brought me presents.

We had
fun playing
party games.

15

After the
games we had
a birthday tea.

We ate lots of
wobbly jelly!

17

My birthday cake
had candles.

My friends sang
"Happy Birthday!"
while I blew the
candles out.

19

Everybody took home some cake and a balloon.

Notes for parents and teachers

READING CORNER has been structured to provide maximum support for new readers. The stories may be used by adults for sharing with young children. Primarily, however, the stories are designed for newly independent readers, whether they are reading these books in bed at night, or in the reading corner at school or in the library.

Starting to read alone can be a daunting prospect. **READING CORNER** helps by providing visual support and repeating words and phrases, while making reading enjoyable. These books will develop confidence in the new reader, and encourage a love of reading that will last a lifetime!

If you are reading this book with a child, here are a few tips:

1. Make reading fun! Choose a time to read when you and the child are relaxed and have time to share the story.

2. Encourage children to reread the story, and to retell the story in their own words, using the illustrations to remind them what has happened.

3. Give praise. Remember that small mistakes need not always be corrected.

READING CORNER covers three grades of early reading ability, with three levels at each grade. Each level has a certain number of words per story, indicated by the number of bars on the spine of the book, to allow you to choose the right book for a young reader:

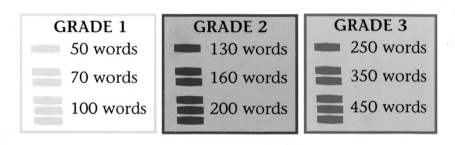

GRADE 1	GRADE 2	GRADE 3
50 words	130 words	250 words
70 words	160 words	350 words
100 words	200 words	450 words